CHURCH
DISCIPLINE

Andrew Wommack

Published in partnership between Andrew Wommack Ministries and Harrison House Publishers.

Woodland Park, CO 80863 - Shippensburg, PA 17257

ISBN 13 TP: 978-1-59548-723-0

For Worldwide Distribution.

1 2 3 4 5 6 / 27 26 25 24

Contents

The subject of church discipline is not pleasant and much confusion about it makes it very difficult to deal with. The vast majority of believers simply avoid it altogether. But that is not the approach the Apostle Paul took.

Paul spent the first four chapters of his letter to the Corinthians dealing with their division over who was their favorite minister. He soundly rebuked such factions and said the believers were supposed to be united in the same mind and the same judgment (1 Cor. 1:10).

Then in the fifth chapter of 1 Corinthians, Paul begins to rebuke the believers for not dealing with the really important matters such as the man who was committing incest with his stepmother.

It is reported commonly that there is fornication among you, and such fornication as is not so much as named among the Gentiles, that one should have his father's wife. And ye are puffed up, and have not rather mourned, that he that hath done this deed might be taken away from among you. For I verily, as absent in body, but present in spirit, have judged already, as though I were present, concerning *him that hath so done this deed, In the name of our Lord Jesus Christ, when ye are gathered together, and my spirit, with the power of our Lord Jesus Christ, To deliver such an one unto Satan for the destruction of the flesh, that the spirit may be saved in the day of the Lord Jesus.*

1 Corinthians 5:1-5

Paul was appalled and said even unbelievers don't live in that type of immorality. While the church was arguing over who was the better preacher, they were allowing this gross sin of incest to thrive in their midst. Isn't this the way it always is?

Those who are way off base major on the minors while ignoring or making light of the really important things. As Jesus put it,

> *Ye blind guides, which strain at a gnat, and swallow a camel.*

Matthew 23:24

> *Thou hypocrite, first cast out the beam out of thine own eye; and then shalt thou see clearly to cast out the mote out of thy brother's eye.*

Matthew 7:5

Today we have people who get incensed over the suffering of a little puppy while promoting killing a child in their mother's womb. They can't tolerate Christian values, but they have no problem at all with drag queens promoting pure evil and doing lewd acts in front of young children. They stand in solidarity with terrorists while chanting slogans about love and tolerance.

The same warning applies to these hypocrites today as the one Isaiah gave to the false prophets of his day when he said in Isaiah 5:20,

> *Woe unto them that call evil good, and good evil; that put darkness for light, and light for darkness; that put bitter for sweet, and sweet for bitter!*

This is happening in epidemic proportions today.

With that as the background, let's see how Paul instructed the believers in Corinth to deal with this man who openly committed incest with his stepmother. Although this is only one example of church discipline, it provides principles that can guide us in dealing with all matters of church discipline.

CHURCH DISCIPLINE IS NOT OPTIONAL

First of all, we need to realize that church discipline is not optional for those who want to follow scripture. Paul was shocked that the believers in Corinth hadn't dealt with this. He said they were puffed up or as the *New Living Translation* says, "*You are so proud of yourselves, but you should be mourning in sorrow and shame. And you should remove this man from your fellowship*" (1 Cor. 5:2).

When Christians don't deal with sin, it is a reason for shame, not pride. We are not only accountable to the Lord for what we do but we have accountability for what we allow too.

There is a segment in traditional wedding vows that says, "If anyone objects to this union, let him speak now or forever hold his peace." If no objection is given, then it is assumed that everyone in attendance is in agreement with what is taking place. In legal terms, this is called "tacit agreement."

In Numbers 30, the Law of Moses said that if a father held his peace when he heard his daughter make a vow, then she would be bound by it. But if he disavowed it on the very day she said it, it would be forgiven her. He had to speak up or else he established her vow.

The same principle was given in Leviticus 19:17-18 where the Lord said loving your neighbor as yourself means rebuking them, regardless of how difficult it is, so they will not live in sin. In Leviticus 20:4-5, the Lord held people guilty if they knew of others who committed idolatry but didn't speak up.

These verses clearly show we have a responsibility to speak up about what's going on around us. Certainly, we can't correct every wrong in the world, but believers are supposed to police fellow believers (1 Cor. 5:12).

TWO WRONGS DON'T MAKE A RIGHT

Just because church discipline has been done incorrectly doesn't absolve us of our responsibility to the Lord and other members of our Christian family to judge one another. Many Christians have been misled by a wrong understanding of Jesus' teaching in Matthew 7:1-2 which says,

Judge not, that ye be not judged. For with what judgment ye judge, ye shall be judged: and with what measure ye mete, it shall be measured to you again.

It's been incorrectly interpreted that Jesus was forbidding judging others. That is not what He was saying at all.

For example, in the case of the man who had committed incest, Paul said he had already judged him (1 Cor. 5:3). All of 1 Corinthians 6 is Paul teaching the Corinthians to judge disputes among themselves instead of going before secular judges.

Paul also commanded the believers in 1 Corinthians 14:29 to judge one another's prophesies to determine if they were accurate. In Revelation 2, Jesus Himself rebuked the pastors of the churches of Pergamos and Thyatira for not judging those who were causing error in their churches.

From these scriptural examples we can see Jesus wasn't speaking against judging others. We have to make judgments every single day of our lives about others and what their motives are. A person would be a fool to take what everyone says at face value. We need godly discernment now more than ever.

Jesus was simply warning against making wrong judgments of others, reminding us that we will be judged by the same standards we use to judge others. Therefore, we need to be certain our judgments are correct.

The *Amplified Bible* translation of Matthew 7:1-2 says,

Do not judge and *criticize and condemn [others unfairly with an attitude of self-righteous superiority as though assuming the office of a judge], so that you will not be judged [unfairly]. For just as you [hypocritically] judge others [when you are sinful and unrepentant], so will you be judged; and in accordance with your standard of measure [used to pass out judgment], judgment will be measured to you.*

So, godly judging isn't wrong and church discipline is not optional. It is necessary and commanded in scripture. However, this is not an occasion for believers to go on a "witch hunt" and become judge and jury of everyone they disagree with. Jesus gave very clear instructions on how to deal with offenses between believers in Matthew 18:15-20.

Some are also "turned off" to church discipline because of the way it has been incorrectly administered. During the Middle Ages, people who disagreed with the Catholic Church were deemed heretics and burned at the stake. In more recent times, the Catholic Church excommunicates those they discipline, which means, according to their rationale, they are doomed to hell without an opportunity to repent.

But Paul made it clear that the judgment he was prescribing for this man who committed incest was redemptive, not punitive. In fact, Paul reveals in his second letter to the Corinthians that the man they turned over to Satan repented and Paul told the believers to receive him back into their fellowship.

> *Sufficient to such a man* is *this punishment, which* was inflicted *of many. So that contrariwise ye* ought *rather to forgive* him, *and comfort* him, *lest perhaps such a one should be swallowed up with overmuch sorrow. Wherefore I beseech you that ye would confirm* your *love toward him.*

> 2 Corinthians 2:6-8

So, regardless of how others have abused this principle of church discipline, there is still a godly reason and way to do this. Just as some abuse disciplining children, likewise, the church has certainly misused and misapplied church discipline in ungodly ways. But we shouldn't refuse to administer discipline to church members because others have done it incorrectly any more than we should never correct children because some abuse that.

CHURCH DISCIPLINE

Paul also made it very clear in 1 Corinthians 5:4 that this discipline was to be done as a church body, not on an individual basis. That's why it's called "church discipline" not "individual discipline." We need the security of the whole body of believers to keep one individual from railroading someone they dislike out of the fellowship of the believers.

Church discipline is not an occasion to vent our wrath on any brother or sister. When done correctly, by the entire body of believers, it is an expression of love with the ultimate goal of restoration.

Scripture prescribes church discipline for the following:

1. Strife between people (Matt. 18:15-20)
2. Disorderly conduct (2 Thess. 3:11-15)
3. Doctrinal errors (1 Tim. 1:20 with 2 Tim. 2:17-18)
4. Sins of immorality (1 Cor. 5)

This instance of turning the man who committed incest over to Satan is the final step in church discipline. Before we get to what that was and how we do it, let's look at the instructions Jesus gave about how to deal with strife between individuals. His instructions, if followed, will keep things from escalating to this final step of turning someone over to Satan.

FOUR STEPS OF CONFLICT RESOLUTION

In Matthew 18:15-20, Jesus gave three steps for dealing with a problem before it reaches the critical fourth step of turning someone over to Satan.

Step 1

Moreover if thy brother shall trespass against thee, go and tell him his fault between thee and him alone: if he shall hear thee, thou hast gained thy brother.

Matthew 18:15

If there is a problem between two individuals, Jesus instructed us to first go to that person alone and talk to them to try to reconcile the differences. This is a critical first step that should always be observed. However, that is seldom how it is done.

Typically, when there's a problem between two people, they usually tell someone else about the problem instead of going directly to the person they are at odds with. This causes multiple problems and plays right into the hands of the devil who uses strife as an inroad of every evil work (Jam. 3:16).

We've come up with very religious sounding ways of justifying why we don't follow Jesus' command. We often say I'm not sure what to do or how to react and I want you to counsel me or pray with me about this situation. That sounds good, but it's not what Jesus told us to do. He said to go to the person who has offended you and talk to them directly.

We should never say anything about a person that we haven't already said to that person!

That would change everything!

Most people dislike personal conflict so much that if they had to talk to the person instead of about that person, they would get over minor offenses. But when we talk about someone, with no accountability to that person, things can get out of hand in a hurry. Plus, if we find out our offense was unjustified, now we have infected another person with our sour attitude.

One of the worst things that has come from social media is people being empowered to say whatever they want without having to personally confront the other person. That produces a harshness and crassness, which wouldn't happen if we had to confront people face to face, as Jesus instructed. I'm sure this is one of the major contributing factors to the rampant disrespect and vitriol in our world today.

I had a person who was very close to me say terrible things about me on social media that they would never have said to my face. They are meek in person but vicious online. That should not be. The lack of face-to-face confrontation is a major contributor to the increased wrath and anger we see exhibited in our society today.

We are not supposed to vent our hurt to anyone or in any form until we have talked directly to the individual involved. That would solve a lot of problems.

One of the problems this would solve is the misinterpretation of another's actions or speech, leading to taking offense when none is intended. Someone could have been joking but you took it seriously. Maybe they were just having a bad day and weren't thinking about how you would take what they said. Maybe you amplified a small thing into something big. Unless you talk about it with the person directly, you won't know.

I actually heard a person criticize a pastor because the pastor walked right by them and didn't speak to them as they usually did. They took that to mean the pastor didn't love them or was upset with them in some way. I told them maybe something happened that totally captivated his attention, and he might not have even noticed you. What if he just got word of someone's death or a problem in the church? Is it possible that he was thinking of someone or something other than you?

If they had gone directly to the pastor instead of me, and asked him if there was a problem, it's possible that the whole situation could have been taken care of with a simple explanation of what the pastor was going through. As Jesus said, we should go directly to them personally and get it straightened out.

I once made a joke about a very good friend of mine. I didn't mean anything by it, but the next day his wife called and asked to see me. She told me her husband had been hurt by what I said. I didn't intend that at all. I loved this guy. It was just foolish talking and jesting, which was inappropriate (Eph. 5:4). I was young and learned a lesson from that, and because his wife came directly to me, I apologized, and we remained friends.

A person may say, "Well, I'm really not sure there is a problem. It might be nothing. Maybe I'm just too sensitive. I don't want to confront them over something that might be nothing." If it isn't big enough for you to confront them over, then you should cast it into the sea of forgetfulness and put up a "No Fishing" sign.

As a former introvert, I've had to deal with a fear of what people think of me. The fear of man is a real snare (Prov. 29:25) and keeps us from operating in God's kind of faith (John 5:44).

I determined a long time ago that if someone has something against me, they are going to have to come and let me know about it. I'm not going to read between the lines and take offense from hints.

I learned this the hard way through an instance where very good friends failed to show up at one of my meetings. Normally they would come hours early so they could get a front row seat and they never missed. One night, however, they weren't there. My mind began to race, wondering what had happened.

I didn't sleep well that night because I was thinking about the situation. The next day I mused on why they weren't there and convinced myself they had gotten offended and were probably mad at me and criticizing me behind my back. I was so upset I was ready to let them have it the next time I saw them.

Then they showed up at my meeting that night in their usual front row seats. They came up and apologized for missing the previous night, but they'd had a death in the family. They said that's the only reason they would ever miss one of my services. I felt like a fool. I had let the devil torment me with negative thoughts for twenty-four hours over something that never happened.

I determined right then that if someone has a problem with me, they are going to have to tell me. I'm not going to let something that may not exist rent space in my mind. I'm going to think the best about people until I know differently.

Also, it's often the case that someone who has been hurt before is walking around with a chip on their shoulder, just daring people to knock it off. They interpret everything through their lens of hurt and pain, which leads to them taking everything wrong when no wrong was intended.

I had a female employee who had come from an abusive marriage that caused her to hate and distrust all men. If a man complimented her on anything, she took it as sexual harassment. She wound up filing a sexual harassment lawsuit against a fellow worker, which she lost because it was frivolous. The problem was with her and not the other person.

If she had gone to the individual whom she perceived was harassing her, she would have learned that there was no sexual harassment intended, and that man could have avoided any further comment that would have aggravated her. It would have nipped the problem in the bud. Instead, she vented to everyone around her and escalated the conflict to a lawsuit and her eventual departure from the ministry.

All of this and more can be prevented if we just do what Jesus told us to do and go directly to anyone who we think has offended us. If we resolve the conflict in this first step, then great. We've maintained our relationship with our brother or sister.

I have one word of caution before we move on to step two. If the other person doesn't know that they have offended you, you need to consider just letting the offense go. That's not true in every situation, but there are times that you need to just cast your care over on the Lord and forget things (1 Pet. 5:7).

I remember when I was a teenager, we had a powerful move of the Spirit in one of our youth services. The Lord touched kids' hearts to forgive and get things right between each other. It was a genuine move of the Lord and there were some relationships restored. Praise the Lord!

But I had one young man come to me in tears, saying he had always hated me. He asked me to forgive him, which I did. That was no problem. I had nothing against him, and as far as I knew, I had never done anything to hurt him. He went away rejoicing.

But then I had to deal with rejection, knowing he had disliked me for years and wondering what he had been saying about me to others. It took a while for me to get over that.

There is no doubt he had been dealing with anger and unforgiveness, which he needed to get rid of. But I didn't have a clue how he had felt about me. In that case, I think that is something he should have dealt with between him and the Lord. As long as he had not spread his criticism of me to others, there was no reason to involve me when I had no clue there was a problem.

But if the conflict is known to both parties, Jesus instructed us to go directly to the other person and confront them alone, before we speak to anyone else about it.

Step 2

> *But if he will not hear* thee, then *take with thee one or two more, that in the mouth of two or three witnesses every word may be established.*

Matthew 18:16

If we follow step one, going directly to the person we're having a problem with, and that doesn't resolve the situation, then step two is to take one or two people with us and confront that person again.

Jesus is not instructing us to confront the individual with a couple of our friends who we have prejudiced with our slant of the problem and are sure to agree with us. Rather, this is referring to what we would call "arbitration" or "mediation".

This involves taking a couple of people who we believe have godly judgment and wisdom and don't "have a dog in this hunt." That is to say, they don't have a prejudice or opinion about who is right and who is wrong. They come to the situation with open minds and hearts and look at the problem objectively.

Often when someone has hurt us, we aren't objective. We've gone over the perceived offense so often in our minds that we have "tunnel vision" and can't see the other person's point of view. When discussing the problem, we often aren't listening to the other person, but are formulating what we will say next to defend our position. That's why these other people—the mediators—are needed.

Also, if the person we confront doesn't respond positively and we have to escalate to the next level, we now have the conflict documented in the mouths of two or three witnesses.

Deuteronomy 19:15 says,

One witness shall not rise up against a man for any iniquity, or for any sin, in any sin that he sinneth: at the mouth of two witnesses, or at the mouth of three witnesses, shall the matter be established.

This was a well-established law that was repeated five other times in scripture and even by Jesus in this very text (Matt. 18:16). Paul also used this scripture in 1 Timothy 5:19. No one should ever be disciplined on the word of just one person.

Paul referred to this principle when he said in 1 Corinthians 5:1 that it was commonly reported that this man had committed incest. This wasn't an accusation leveled by just one person. Everyone knew it was true.

So, taking a couple of other people with you will either help you to understand the situation through the eyes of impartial arbitrators and bring reconciliation, or it will establish the error of the other person in the mouths of two or three witnesses as the scripture dictates.

Step 3

And if he shall neglect to hear them, tell it *unto the church...*

Matthew 18:17a

If the first two steps have been completed as prescribed by Jesus in Matthew 18:15-16, the next step is to bring the problem before the whole church for judgment (Matt. 18:17). Now the sin isn't just between a couple of individuals; it becomes a church matter.

Paul said in 1 Corinthians 5:11 that this discipline should be for serious things like fornication, covetousness, idolatry, railings, drunkenness, and extortion. In 1 Timothy 1:20 along with 2 Timothy 2:16-17, we read that Paul turned two people over to Satan because of doctrinal issues. And 2 Thessalonians 3:11-15 instructed the believers to withdraw from anyone who wouldn't work and just "mooched" off others.

Petty issues such as comments about a person's weight, dress, or hairstyle don't warrant bringing the dispute before the whole church. As long as carnal Christians exist, petty problems will exist. Mature Christians must rise above these minor differences and walk in love, regardless of what others do.

The first two steps that Jesus gave in Matthew 18:15-16 can be followed today by anyone who is sincere and truly looking to reconcile, and not just get even. But steps three and four are much harder to accomplish, not because it's not the proper path to follow, but because this involves the church executing church discipline. That rarely happens today.

Paul went on to share in 1 Corinthians 6 that it was to the believers' shame that they didn't resolve their differences among themselves but went before unbelievers to judge their problems. Paul said it would be better to suffer wrong than for

Christians to look to the judicial system to right their wrongs (1 Cor. 6:7).

That's because he was more concerned about his Christian witness than he was about any wrong done to him. Paul would not run the risk of bringing disgrace to the name of Christ just so he could get justice. What would the unbelievers think if they saw Christians at odds with each other? Didn't the Lord say that it was our love for other believers that would make the world know we are His disciples (John 13:35 and 17:22-23)? Paul would not compromise his witness, even if that meant he might be taken advantage of.

Imagine two Christians living next door to each other. One of them puts a fence up but the other neighbor believes the fence encroaches on their property. The Christian who feels wronged should first go to the other Christian and see if they can work it out.

If that doesn't resolve the issue, they should take a couple of other believers with them to mediate the disagreement. If that doesn't work, they should either just live with it for love's sake or bring it before the church and let the church settle the issue. But sadly, that would not be the way this would play out with most Christians today.

Brother will take Christian brother to court, "*and that before the unbelievers*" (1 Cor. 6:6). Paul said,

Now therefore there is utterly a fault among you, because ye go to law one with another. Why do ye not rather take wrong? why do ye not rather suffer yourselves *to be defrauded? Nay, ye do wrong, and defraud, and that* your *brethren.*

1 Corinthians 6:7-8

There are very few Christians today who put God and their witness for Him ahead of their personal gain. And there are very few churches that would accept the responsibility Jesus spoke of in Matthew 18:17 where the church would get involved in disputes among its members. Most pastors would ask, "Why don't you take them to court?"

So, steps one and two of Jesus' instructions can be implemented today by anyone who is committed to the Lord and truly wants what is best, not just what's best for themselves. But the next two steps depend on the cooperation of the church and that's hard to come by today.

I've heard of a group of Christian lawyers who have tried to step up in the absence of churches taking the lead in this. They will actually judge from a biblical point of view between Christians who have disputes with each other. They make the parties sign a legal document that they will abide by the decision they hand down, but they are seeking to follow Jesus' command to resolve differences within the body of believers. That should be done by the church.

Anyone who has followed steps one and two and then approached the average church to continue the process would not be welcomed. Very few churches would take the responsibility of judging between their church members. And even if you can find a church that would do that and proceed to the final step of disfellowshipping a person because of their sin, all that person would have to do is go across the street and join another church. Thus, the church discipline would be diluted.

The schism in the body of Christ today has lessened any discipline that an individual church body could mete out. As I'll explain in the next section, the ultimate step in church discipline is withdrawing from the offending person spiritually and physically. That's what Paul told the Corinthians to do (1 Cor. 5:5).

In Paul's day, there was only one church per city. Believers met in many locations because they met in homes, and one house could not contain all the believers. But they were all in unity and under one leadership, although they were in different locations. That's not true today. There are churches located across the street from other churches with no communication between them.

So, to withdraw fellowship from any believer over their error would not necessarily cut them off from Christian fellowship and support. They could just walk across the street and be accepted into a new fellowship. They would not be affected in the same way as in Paul's day.

Nevertheless, if the situation is elevated to the place where the problem comes before the church, and the church rules in favor of one party against the other, then the offending party has to repent or be disfellowshipped from the body of believers. That is the next and final step.

Step 4

> *…but if he neglect to hear the church, let him be unto thee as an heathen man and a publican.*

> Matthew 18:17b

Step four is where the individual has not repented, and therefore, the church treats them as a heathen man or a publican. This is the same thing that Paul spoke of in 1 Corinthians 5:5, where he turned that man over to Satan for the destruction of the flesh so the spirit might be saved in the day of judgment.

This is not speaking of damning his soul to hell.

When the Catholic Church excommunicates someone, they consider that as condemning that person to hell because Catholics believe your eternal salvation is tied to the Catholic Church. Therefore, if they kick you out of the Church, they are eliminating the possibility of you going to heaven. That's not true.

As I've already shared, this man who committed incest in 1 Corinthians 5:1 and was turned over to Satan for the destruction of his flesh, repented and was received back into the church's fellowship (2 Cor. 2:6-7).

This action was redemptive and not punitive. Jesus said to treat him as a heathen man or a publican (sinner). We aren't supposed to hate sinners, but we are not supposed to have the same relationship with those outside of the body of Christ as with our brothers and sisters in the Lord.

As Paul said in 2 Corinthians 6:14-18,

Be ye not unequally yoked together with unbelievers: for what fellowship hath righteousness with unrighteousness? and what communion hath light with darkness? And what concord hath Christ with Belial? or what part hath he that believeth with an infidel? And what agreement hath the temple of God with idols? for ye are the temple of the living God; as God hath said, I will dwell in them, and walk in them; *and I will be their God, and they shall be my people. Wherefore come out from among them, and be ye separate, saith the Lord, and touch not the unclean* thing; *and I will receive you, And will be a Father unto you, and ye shall be my sons and daughters, saith the Lord Almighty.*

We are to be in the world but not of the world (John 17:15-16). Although we show the love of God to those outside the body of Christ, we don't embrace them and their values the way we do fellow believers. The love between fellow members of Christ's body should be special. We should love and support each other through prayer and fellowship in a way that makes a huge difference.

To illustrate, I pastored a very small church in Seagoville, Texas, for two years. We only had a dozen or so people coming to church, but we were a tight-knit group. We prayed for each other fervently and would do anything for each other.

One of the ladies in the church was a schoolteacher who was very outspoken with her Christian witness. She had been criticized by her principal several times and threatened with losing her job if she didn't tone it down. We prayed with her about this multiple times.

We had an agreement in this church that if someone was in trouble, all they had to do was ask the Lord to speak to the other members and we would drop what we were doing and pray for them at that very moment. One day I was impressed to pray for this lady and couldn't wait to come to church that night to find out what had happened. It turned out other church members had the same thing happen to them.

She shared that she was called to the principal's office over the loudspeaker. She knew she was in trouble, so as she walked to the principal's office, she asked the Lord to speak to us to intercede for her. When she got to the principal, he just looked at her, and said, "Ah, go back to your room!" She knew she dodged a bullet, and she knew it was because of her brothers' and sisters' intercession. That's the way the body of Christ is supposed to function. We are a body, not just individual members. If one member suffers, we all feel it (1 Cor. 12:26).

But in the absence of that kind of unity and care for each other today, withdrawing fellowship from a fellow believer has minimal impact. If we aren't in a truly loving, and close relationship with other believers, depriving them of something they never had doesn't mean much.

Therefore, this final step of turning someone over to Satan only works if the body of believers has been functioning the way scripture admonishes us to. If there isn't this love and care and intercession for each other, this church discipline is minimized. Add to this the schism that exists in the body of Christ today, where there are many churches in the same area with no relationship with each other, and any individual who has been disfellowshipped can just go somewhere else to find fellowship. The church isn't functioning today as it was in Paul's day.

In the early church, it cost a lot to be a Christian. Up until the third century, they used to have potential converts go through a lengthy process called a catechism before they would let them become a part of a local body. This was because they could be put to death for their profession of Jesus as their Lord, and they wanted them to know what they were signing up for.

As a result of the persecution, the believers met daily from house to house. Their assemblies were actually called love feasts (Jude 1:12 NKJV). They were closer to their brothers and sisters in the Lord than their own flesh and blood in many cases. That is still true today in some cases, but sadly, church is just a one-hour-per-week meeting for most people who claim the name of Christ. There is not the intimacy today that there was in the early church, and therefore, it doesn't have the same impact to withdraw what one never had.

When I pastored in Seagoville, Texas, at the church I mentioned earlier, we actually turned a person over to Satan. There was a young man who went to a local Baptist church but was a dope dealer. He came to a meeting I held with his youth group, and forty out of forty-two kids received the baptism of the Holy Spirit. He was one of them. It was awesome!

However, when they went back to their local Baptist church, the feathers hit the fan. The pastor didn't believe in the baptism of the Holy Spirit or speaking in tongues, and he came out against it very hard. He met with the teens and their parents and told them this was strictly of the devil. The vast majority of those kids wound up renouncing the experience. But not this young man. He stuck with it over the summer months. I spent a lot of time with him, and he was receiving revelation directly from the Lord. It was great.

But when he went back to school, all his Baptist friends ostracized him and would not even talk to him. The only people who would have anything to do with him were his old doper friends.

By Christmas, he had walked away from the Lord and went back to doing dope and in the next year moved in with a girl.

This close-knit group of believers in the church at Seagoville prayed for him constantly. We bound the devil off his life and prayed that the Lord would make His love real to him, regardless of what he was doing.

One day I visited this young man. I told him how much we missed him and that we prayed for him all the time. I told him that after tasting of the goodness of the Lord, as he had, I knew he must be miserable. He shocked me by saying that wasn't true at all. He admitted that before he was born again, he was so condemned he could hardly stand it. But now, even though he knew what he was doing was sinful, it was different. He still felt the love of the Lord and wasn't depressed at all.

I couldn't believe that at first. It just didn't make sense that he could be living in open sin and yet not reap the results. I shared that with the church body that evening and we spent the whole night praying about this and discussing what we should do. We came to the conclusion that it was our prayers that were keeping him from reaping what he was sowing. We were enabling his lifestyle of sin by our prayers.

After much discussion and prayer, and as a church body, we decided to withdraw our prayers and let him reap what he was sowing. We didn't do that in order to punish him but in hopes that he would turn from his sin when it started hurting him. This is exactly what Paul did with the man in 1 Corinthians 5 who had committed incest.

Early the next morning, this young man was knocking on my door. He said, "What did you all do last night? I was fine before your visit yesterday, but now I'm miserable again. I know it was what you and the other believers did at church last night."

What we did was to turn him over to Satan for the destruction of his flesh so his soul could be saved in the day of judgment. We withdrew our intercession and actually retained his sins unto him. That's what Jesus said we could do in John 20:23.

> *Whose soever sins ye remit, they are remitted unto them;* and *whose soever* sins *ye retain, they are retained.*

We can remit people's sins through our intercession which keeps the devil at bay. Remitting sins is not forgiving sins. Only God can forgive sins, but remittance has to do with the effects sin has upon a person. A person may be doing drugs or committing sexual sins that open them up to danger and all kinds of diseases, but through the intercession of believers, we can stop the destruction Satan wants to do to them.

However, if a believer is using the intercession of other believers to keep themselves from experiencing the wages of their sin (Rom. 6:23), there comes a time to retain their sins unto them. This is simply withdrawing the prayers and intercession which has been protecting them from the devil's snare. Retaining their sins is simply letting them reap what they are sowing.

This is only a last resort and should not be done lightly. That's why Jesus said this was only to be done after bringing the matter before the whole church. This prevents an individual from doing this to get even with someone for selfish reasons. That should never be the case. This church discipline is to be redemptive.

Paul told the Corinthians that they were not to keep company with any believer who was a fornicator, covetous, an idolater, a railer, a drunkard, or an extortioner. He even forbade them to eat with anyone living like that (1 Cor. 5:11). All of that was in the context of turning someone over to Satan.

Paul turned Hymenaeus and Alexander over to Satan in 1 Timothy 1:20. In 2 Timothy 2:16-18,

Paul said these two men were saying that the resurrection had passed, which overthrew the faith of some. So, Paul executed judgment on these people for gross doctrinal errors.

In 2 Thessalonians 3:6, Paul told the Thessalonians to withdraw from every brother who walks disorderly. Paul went on to specify that he was talking about people who wouldn't work and just mooched off other members of the body. He gave instructions that if someone would not work, neither should they eat (2 Thess. 3:10).

This withdrawal from someone, physically and spiritually, might not seem like much of a deterrent to us today, but that's because we don't have the close relationships and intercession for our fellow members of Christ's body that they had in Paul's day. Division has been accepted and even promoted in many cases today.

However, in those instances where being a part of a vital church and drawing on the intercession of others is important to an individual, this church discipline can be very effective. Under those circumstances, the love and support of our Christian family can be a deal changer. I've seen a number of people protected from what could have been death through my intercession. We should be loving each other and praying for each other much more than we do.

Let me caution you again that this church discipline should not be done individually or lightly. To turn someone over to the one who only comes to steal, kill, and destroy (John 10:10) is a drastic step. This could lead to all kinds of destruction, including death. It should only be done for the major cases we've already laid out and it should not be done without the input of the church leadership.

One of the things I pray will come from this brief teaching is that believers will gain a greater understanding of how important Christian fellowship and intercession are. To a large degree, today's believers have already been turned over to Satan because the body hasn't been loving and interceding for each other as the scriptures admonish us to.

We are fighting without the advantages that corporate faith and support could afford. Many believers are fighting alone. There are many battles that need the synergy of the whole church body. Ministry leaders need to train and prepare us to fight as a unit. We will have much greater victories if we do.

The Lord commands a special blessing on unity (Ps. 133), and when the body of Christ unifies for or against someone, supernatural power is released.

In context, this is what Jesus was speaking about in Matthew 18:18-20 which says,

> *Verily I say unto you, Whatsoever ye shall bind on earth shall be bound in heaven: and whatsoever ye shall loose on earth shall be loosed in heaven. Again I say unto you, That*

*if two of you shall agree on earth as touching
any thing that they shall ask, it shall be done
for them of my Father which is in heaven.
For where two or three are gathered together
in my name, there am I in the midst of them.*

These verses are often used to teach about our authority to bind and loose the devil, which is correct. But in context, this is speaking about binding or loosing the devil through our intercession. That's the context.

Jesus said these things right after He gave instructions about the four steps of resolving conflict. If the individual won't repent and abide by the judgment of the church, the church is to withdraw from that person and retain their sins unto them (Matt. 18:17).

Then Jesus said, "*Whatsoever ye shall bind on earth shall be bound in heaven: and whatsoever ye shall loose on earth shall be loosed in heaven*" (Matt. 18:18). He was speaking about executing church discipline and assuring them that whatever judgment was meted out by the church would also be enforced in heaven. For when two or three are gathered together, there He is in their midst. This was still dealing with church discipline.

So, the body of Christ has supernatural power at our disposal to deal with fellow believers who stray from the truth. But it doesn't operate automatically. First, we must come together in love and start interceding for one another. Then, if a brother or sister departs from the faith, these steps of church discipline will be a huge deterrent and, hopefully, bring them back to submission to the Lord.

I pray the Lord gives you understanding of this and leads you into a greater love and unity for your fellow believers.

> *By this shall all* men *know that ye are my disciples, if ye have love one to another.*
>
> John 13:35

Let it be. Amen!

FURTHER STUDY

If you enjoyed this booklet and would like to learn more about some of the things I've shared, I suggest my teachings:

- *Church Discipline CD*
- *God's Kind of Love Through You*

These teachings are available either free of charge at **awmi.net** or for purchase in various formats at **awmi.net/store**.

Receive Jesus as Your Savior

Choosing to receive Jesus Christ as your Lord and Savior is the most important decision you'll ever make!

God's Word promises, *"That if thou shalt confess with thy mouth the Lord Jesus, and shalt believe in thine heart that God hath raised him from the dead, thou shalt be saved. For with the heart man believeth unto righteousness; and with the mouth confession is made unto salvation"* (Rom. 10:9–10). *"For whosoever shall call upon the name of the Lord shall be saved"* (Rom. 10:13). By His grace, God has already done everything to provide salvation. Your part is simply to believe and receive.

Pray out loud: "Jesus, I acknowledge that I've sinned and need to receive what you did for the forgiveness of my sins. I confess that You are my Lord and Savior. I believe in my heart that God raised You from the dead. By faith in Your Word, I receive salvation now. Thank You for saving me."

The very moment you commit your life to Jesus Christ, the truth of His Word instantly comes to pass in your spirit. Now that you're born again, there's a brand-new you!

Please contact us and let us know that you've prayed to receive Jesus as your Savior. We'd like to send you some free materials to help you on your new journey. Call our Helpline: **719-635-1111** (available 24 hours a day, seven days a week) to speak to a staff member who is here to help you understand and grow in your new relationship with the Lord.

Welcome to your new life!

Receive the Holy Spirit

As His child, your loving heavenly Father wants to give you the supernatural power you need to live a new life. *"For every one that asketh receiveth; and he that seeketh findeth; and to him that knocketh it shall be opened…how much more shall* your *heavenly Father give the Holy Spirit to them that ask him?"* (Luke 11:10–13).

All you have to do is ask, believe, and receive! Pray this: "Father, I recognize my need for Your power to live a new life. Please fill me with Your Holy Spirit. By faith, I receive it right now. Thank You for baptizing me. Holy Spirit, You are welcome in my life."

Some syllables from a language you don't recognize will rise up from your heart to your mouth (1 Cor. 14:14). As you speak them out loud by faith, you're releasing God's power from within and building yourself up in the spirit (1 Cor. 14:4). You can do this whenever and wherever you like.

It doesn't really matter whether you felt anything or not when you prayed to receive the Lord and His Spirit. If you believed in your heart that you received, then God's Word promises you did. *"Therefore I say unto you, What things soever ye desire, when ye pray, believe that ye receive* them, *and ye shall have* them"* (Mark 11:24). God always honors His Word—believe it!

We would like to rejoice with you, pray with you, and answer any questions to help you understand more fully what has taken place in your life!

Please contact us to let us know that you've prayed to be filled with the Holy Spirit and to request the book *The New You & the Holy Spirit.* This book will explain in more detail about the benefits of being filled with the Holy Spirit and speaking in tongues. Call our Helpline: **719-635-1111** (available 24 hours a day, seven days a week).

About the Author

Andrew Wommack's life was forever changed the moment he encountered the supernatural love of God on March 23, 1968. As a renowned Bible teacher and author, Andrew has made it his mission to change the way the world sees God.

Andrew's vision is to go as far and deep with the Gospel as possible. His message goes far through the *Gospel Truth* television program, which is available to over half the world's population. The message goes deep through discipleship at Charis Bible College, headquartered in Woodland Park, Colorado. Founded in 1994, Charis has campuses across the United States and around the globe.

Andrew also has an extensive library of teaching materials in print, audio, and video. More than 200,000 hours of free teachings can be accessed at **awmi.net**.

Contact Information

Andrew Wommack Ministries, Inc.

PO Box 3333
Colorado Springs, CO 80934-3333
info@awmi.net
awmi.net

Helpline: 719-635-1111 (available 24/7)

Charis Bible College

info@charisbiblecollege.org
844-360-9577
CharisBibleCollege.org

For a complete list of all of our offices,
visit **awmi.net/contact-us**.

Connect with us on social media.

There's more on the website!

Discover FREE teachings, testimonies, and more by scanning the QR code.

Continue to grow in the Word of God! You'll be blessed!

ANDREW WOMMACK MINISTRIES

Your monthly giving makes the greatest kingdom impact.

When you give, you make an impact in the kingdom that lasts for generations. Your generosity enables our phone ministers to answer calls 24/7. Your support is also expanding Charis Bible College and allowing *The Gospel Truth* to reach an even wider global audience. You do this and more through your giving each month!

Become a Grace Partner today!
the QR code or call our Helpline at 719-635-1111 and select option five for Partnership.

Andrew's LIVING COMMENTARY BIBLE SOFTWARE

Andrew Wommack's *Living Commentary* Bible study software is a user-friendly, downloadable program. It's like reading the Bible with Andrew at your side, sharing his revelation with you verse by verse.

Main features:

- Bible study software with a grace-and-faith perspective
- Over 26,000 notes by Andrew on verses from Genesis through Revelation
- *Matthew Henry's Concise Commentary*
- 12 Bible versions
- 2 concordances: *Englishman's Concordance* and *Strong's Concordance*
- 2 dictionaries: *Collaborative International Dictionary* and *Holman's Dictionary*
- Atlas with biblical maps
- Bible and *Living Commentary* statistics
- Quick navigation, including history of verses
- Robust search capabilities (for the Bible and Andrew's notes)
- "Living" (i.e., constantly updated and expanding)
- Ability to create personal notes

Whether you're new to studying the Bible or a seasoned Bible scholar, you'll gain a deeper revelation of the Word from a grace-and-faith perspective.

Purchase Andrew's *Living Commentary* today at **awmi.net/living**, and grow in the Word with Andrew.

Item code: 8350

ANDREW WOMMACK MINISTRIES

CHARIS
BIBLE COLLEGE

God has **more** for you.

Are you longing to find your God-given purpose? At Charis Bible College you will establish a firm foundation in the Word of God and receive hands-on ministry experience to **find, follow,** and **fulfill** your purpose.

Scan the QR code for a free Charis teaching!

CharisBibleCollege.org
Admissions@awmcharis.com
(844) 360-9577

Change your life. **Change the world.**

www.ingramcontent.com/pod-product-compliance
Lightning Source LLC
Chambersburg PA
CBHW071638040426
42452CB00009B/1677